phases

by
courtney raf

preface

i've been writing this book my entire life.

this book is a collection of poems, diary entries, and emails between a friend and i.

the diary entries are marked with a date, but not always a day. 20 year old me apparently didn't think the day was important. the emails are marked with a timestamp.

i was born in 1992 - so that gives you an idea of how old i was when each of these was written.

i like to think of the diary entries as my first poems. even though you're getting a very small excerpt from each entry, it still tells a story of who i was during that phase of my life. seven year old me was very wise.

think of each page as an entirely new chapter.

you'll find plenty of blank space throughout the entire book.

use it. write it all down.

what is 'it'? i don't know. but you do.

let your thoughts pour out of you like rain from a storm, and sail oceans.

april 20, 2010

i always have a lot of thoughts in my head.
i just forget to write them down.

so i'll start now.

january 11, 2017 2:16pm

i miss riding the school bus and getting picked on
and not having bills to pay.

her bones were made of flowers,
delicate and rare.

but roots so deep and haunting,
with strength beyond compare.

do you think the wind is on its way to us?

or is it simply passing through?

i'm not scared.

because being haunted by you would be the most alive i've felt my entire life.

january 13, 2017 1:20pm

i rewatched season 6 because i love when ann leaves.

december 1, 2000

you act cool too much!

you talk about 3am as if it was more
than just a number
that your clock recognizes.

you are the moon
that keeps my raging tides at ease.

june 27, 2010

i couldn't sleep the other night, so i watched the sun rise.
is that what you see every morning?

our souls have the ability to fall in love with places long before we arrive.

december 8, 2010

i just wish i had a plane ticket to france.

once i felt the weight of your hand in mine,
i felt the weight of the world leave my shoulders.

you see that? right over there.
those aren't the clouds covering the rays of the sun.
that's the sun pushing through the grey of the clouds.

september 2, 2004

i am going into 7th grade. i am really nervous and don't feel like going to school, but it beats being home alone, i guess.

oh what it is to wake before the sun

to capture the stars, before the day has won.

as the dust dances with the sun across the room,

i pray these moments never end too soon.

march 10, 2020

my heart is heavy, but it's also growing and
i think that's the most important thing.

september 6, 2004

i just don't no!!! i dunno anymore.

and what a frightening idea,
that the only thing keeping my heart beating
is the sound of you breathing next to me.

crickets will sing the night away
and a blanket of stars will ask you to stay.

may 11, 2016 4:37pm

it's all such a really weird process. but i guess that means
we're adults.

i want to write you.

over and over again.

i want to feel the weight of the pages i fill
on my chest in place of you.

over and over again.

pebbles will drift from ocean to shore
and leave each wave always wanting more.

october, 2012

i'm running out of things to write.

january 1, 2011

who cares when it was said, as long as it's out in the
world to be read.

take my words and never let them

slip through your hands like sand.

may they become the tallest mountains,

and when you fall

a place to land.

march 14, 2016 3:27pm

this is like when we would sit on our beds at our parent's house and talk on msn and dream about the future.

now we're in the future!

and the stars whisper to the moon,

don't go, don't fade away.

and the scariest part of life is that
the hours turn into days
days into years

and all along you hoped that one minute
could last a lifetime.

september, 2012

this brings me to problem number one - i met a boy.

where the light collides with darkness
at the very dawn of day,

that's where you'll always find me,
and i'll never stray away.

september 4, 2004

i just got done eating, so now i have the hiccups.

the strength in your heart will always remain,
as petals fall from flowers like rain.

the beauty in your heart is never to blame,
as petals fall from flowers like rain.

it's tragic, really.

burying our secrets in an unmarked grave.

december 8, 2010

i'm just dreaming out loud for now, but not forever.

as raindrops race their way down glass,
we realize how fast time does pass.

july 14, 2016 3:30pm

pokemon was amazing.

september 2, 2004

today went pretty well, i guess.

as you dance around to 'bette davis eyes',
   you've got the world in your hands

and it's no surprise.

and i haven't figured out yet if the aching in my bones is from your words or the storm rolling in.

but i guess you are the storm.

imagine the picture you would create
if every word you spoke
was equivalent to that of a
paint brush stroke.

the marks you leave go beyond
just imprints of your footsteps
in the

snow.

july 15, 2010

everything is changing, i just can't get used to it.

when i was younger, my family and
i would catch fireflies late at night.

we would put them in jars and
watch them try to drown
the darkness with their light.

we always let them go though.
we never kept them locked up in jars.

i think people are like that too.
keep them locked up long enough

and

you'll only watch them burn out.

and i like to think that the rolling fog was just
the earth below us pouring out its

darkest secrets.

october, 2012

then again, i'm not the nicest person in the world.

i didn't know how to say goodbye.

you weren't mine to say goodbye to.

it was selfish to say hello. because

i didn't know how to say goodbye.

i didn't want to say goodbye.

may 19, 2016 4:40pm

we should just be homeless in santa barbara and live on the beach like we planned.

i wish the presence of you next to my bed
consisted of more than just an image of your face
in a picture frame.

do not speak a word just yet,

as moonbeams trace your silhouette.

february 17, 2017 12:49pm

i was doing really well until about 10 mins ago.

the taste of your words,
so bittersweet.

hold on to hope that our souls
meet.

november 17, 2016 2:51pm

i really do want to meet her.
or will there be too much evil in one room?

it could have been the sunlight hitting her eyes
that gave the illusion of fire,

but i swore i saw a spark.

july 29, 2010

i hope heaven's amazing. it's ok down here.
could be better, i guess.

but we'll always have early mornings as we watch
the sun and the moon fight for the sky.

do not suffocate those memories
by putting them in a glass bottle
and throwing them to sea.

drown yourself in their comfort.

december, 2012

it is now december and a lot has happened since august.
i managed to fall in love, get my tongue pierced, and
commit some unmentionable crimes.

and the letters of your name,
flow effortlessly through each vein.

september, 2012

by the end of this entry, i need to have a decision made.

i didn't need to hear it.

i didn't need to hear the waves to know they were
crashing at my feet.

i could feel it.

it's all the same.

july 29, 2010

i used to know exactly who i was, and now, i'm not so
sure.

trust in your soul the same way
as the winds who do not ask

in which direction to blow.

we'll watch the same moon in the sky and that is enough.

it is the closest i can ever be to you.

so that is enough.

a slow love.

one that sleeps in on rainy sunday mornings.
one that ignites a flame that quietly flickers and burns.
one that forgets what day it is because its only concern is
watching the moon rise each night.

a slow love.

it's the person that i am when he's around. i can feel that fire in me that burned out a long time ago, spark again.

i just hope i don't burn to ash.

you are not your past

or those tiny pieces of broken

glass.

and the waves told secrets,
only the shore could understand.

and as the sun sets, my thoughts rise.

the shape of our hearts is always changing.
leaving behind pieces
and picking up new ones as we go.

but it keeps beating.

september 6, 2016 4:00pm

i hate waiting for anything.

if your pen ever meets that piece of paper,
i hope each drop of ink
and each torn page

remembers me.

in fields of wildflowers,
i would lay with you for hours.

october 22, 2010

there's something about the cold weather that makes me feel
safe.

running from myself was an understatement.
it became a race.

would i burn a hole in the soles of my shoes

or in the soul attached to these heavy bones first?

december 12, 2010

i'm hungry for adventure.

our ghosts will haunt the people we were,
as our previous lives turn into a blur.

may 20, 2016 4:20pm

i used to just type nonsense in word on my computer to act like i was doing something.

i crave mystery.

and to know the pattern of your beating heart.

july 15, 2010

i open the blinds in your room every day. even on a cloudy day.

shadows are cast,
but not without some kind of light.

your life has been built,
but not without some kind of fight.

and in the darkness, everything will be alright.

where the sun meets the wildflowers,
that's where i'll be.

september, 2012

it's ok to want things.

july 29, 2010

there's mold in my fruit, great.

how jealous am i of the rays of the sun,

that brush your skin when each day has begun.

april 20, 2016 4:54pm

i cannot wait until the weekend. i'm going to relax and
apartment shop by myself. and probably watch jurassic park
for the billionth time.

some light can guide you,
but some light can blind you.

november, 2012

it doesn't even matter how i'm going to get there,
i'm just going to do it.

like grains of sand,
you drift away from the touch of
the smallest winds.

october 22, 2010

i was walking into work the other day and i saw this little girl
run and jump into a pile of leaves. she found so much
excitement in something so little. i forgot what that feels like.

and we will watch the cycles of the moon,
and count the sun's rays each afternoon.

december 12, 2010

i'm so effing cold right now.

you held your words down with a paperweight,
but not letting them go could be a mistake.

because listening to those old songs lets me know that there are still pieces of you passing through.

even if it's just in music notes.

august 28, 2010

i really can't wait until i move to new york.

i wish these walls could play back all that they've seen,
so i could see you in more than just my dream.

grey skies and sunsets remind me of you,

it's never goodbye, just see you soon.

september 20, 2010

time is our enemy. it steals from us memories we can't get back.
it haunts me like the ticking of the clock on the wall in the
hospital that night.

november, 2012

i have to stop pretending like i'm made of stone.

january 14, 2017 9:47pm

i just feel like i'm living day by day and i hate that.
like, nothing is really happening. idk, i'm just bored.

like paper lanterns that flicker in the dark,
and whisper your secrets with every spark.

september 28, 2011

wish me luck with life.

how cruel to discover a connection like that with someone you
can't spend more than a couple of

daydreams

with.

you are the ink stains on my skin,

you are the fire i hold within.

december 8, 2010

i don't ever want to settle down.

our souls were dancing soft and slow, to static on the radio.

september 4, 2004

note2self: sry bout messy handwriting.

and the pines will be our guide,
as we race the raging tide.

september 6, 2016 3:05pm

i'm resetting my life this week.

you smelled of books and you looked like dreams,

but your pages were blank and

you were bursting at the seams.

hey

me too

it only took a few sunsets before she learned to see the stars at night instead of just darkness.

may 24, 2016 3:18pm

it's a pattern i fear will never cease
– that sounded pretty poetic of me.

we climbed vines that grew buildings tall,
with the grasp of freedom to catch our fall.

my lips, they stain your neck.

and i wish it was a reflection of the full moon and the way it lights the sea.

but no. just like the moon. this is a phase. and soon, the sea will not glisten. and you will only bring out darkness in me.

her demons. they did not come from darkness.
and that is what makes them so poisonous.

july 27, 2010

i wish i had the guts to say things out loud.
maybe someday i will, but not today.

i caught myself missing you and that moment,
long before it had even passed.

january 1, 2011

people come into your life to change it, positive or not.

july 25, 2016 4:19pm

it's 2016, you'd think they would get it all figured out by now
and our phones wouldn't act like babies when
a little water (or milk) gets near them.

you come with a love like a sunday afternoon,
that always ends too soon.

july 23, 2010

that doesn't really make any sense, but then again, what does?

december 8, 2010

i wish i could write songs, or poetry at least.

even in the quietest of nights,

i can still hear your thoughts running into mine.

number by letter, it's hard to remember
the sound of your voice,
how you left was your choice.

as our shadows dance in the rain, i return to you again.

july 29, 2010

when the wind chimes blow from gusts of wind,
it feels like you're talking to me.

you were adventure and i was direction,

we guided our lives with chaos and affection.

april 8, 2016 1:22pm

i'm wearing a dirty flannel today. i wish i had a lint roller.

september 2, 2004

anyway, i better go do something.

sometimes when i close my eyes,
i confuse the sound of my beating heart
with my longing to hear your footsteps.

and yet, the view i long for most from
the passenger seat window,
is simply your faded finger prints on the glass
you left behind.

if the skies can cry,
so can you.
if time can lose its track,
so can you.
and if the stars can still shine years after they burn out,
so can you.

march 14, 2016 2:33pm

we both have work emails! how cool are we??

i will not put back together all of your broken pieces,
but i will hold them and keep them close to my heart.
sometimes we need to be reminded that not all that is broken
needs to be fixed.

listen to the sky.

you can see the moon during the day sometimes

for a reason.

i counted the seconds in between each breath as you
walked towards me.

i counted the seconds in between each heartbeat as you
walked away from me.

most days my heart is screaming at you to stay.
but all you see is my chest as it quietly and quickly
moves up and down with each beat.

as it quietly and quickly moves up and down with each
scream.

december 18, 2010

it's those moments where i actually know i'm alive because i
can feel something. it's pain, but i feel something.

april 20, 2010

what's it going to be like when time starts to pass and
i grow old and you're
forever young?

BUCKET LIST 2012
number 13. write a book.

@courtneyraf3

Made in the USA
Monee, IL
22 April 2020